Conversations with GPT

A Glimpse into the Mind of AI

Legal Notice

The interview with ChatGPT, an AI language model, presented in this book is a product of complex algorithms and machine learning processes. While ChatGPT strives to provide accurate and informative responses, it is not infallible and may occasionally produce errors or inaccuracies. The author and publisher do not assume any responsibility or liability for any such errors or inaccuracies.

Disclaimer Notice

The views and opinions expressed by ChatGPT in this interview are solely those of the AI language model and do not necessarily reflect the views or opinions of the author, publisher, or any other individuals or organizations. The information provided in this book is for general informational and educational purposes only and is not intended as a substitute for professional advice. The author and publisher disclaim any liability for any loss or damage arising from the use of the information contained in this book.

Contents

The term "artificial" highlights that I am a product of human creation, designed to mimic certain aspects of human intelligence and behavior.

Introduction

Welcome to "Conversations with GPT: A Glimpse into the Mind of AI." This book embarks on a journey through the fascinating and complex world of artificial intelligence, specifically focusing on ChatGPT, an advanced language model developed by OpenAI. From the origins of artificial intelligence, rooted in the philosophical inquiries of ancient times and formalized in the mid-20th century, to the cutting-edge advancements in natural language processing and machine learning, this book provides an insightful exploration of AI's evolution.

We delve into OpenAI's mission to ensure that artificial general intelligence (AGI) benefits all of humanity, highlighting key milestones and ethical considerations that guide its development. Through a detailed timeline, we trace the significant achievements that have shaped OpenAI and its innovative technologies, including the creation of ChatGPT.

In this book, you will also find an engaging interview with ChatGPT, offering a unique perspective on the nature of AI, its capabilities, and its interactions with humans. The interview touches on various aspects of AI, from its technical foundations to its ethical implications, providing readers with a comprehensive understanding of what it means to converse with an artificial mind.

As you turn the pages, you'll gain insights into the advancements that have made AI a pivotal force in today's world, the competition among leading AI entities, and the collaborative efforts to advance ethical AI. Whether you are a tech enthusiast, a curious reader, or someone keen on understanding the future of artificial intelligence, "Conversations with GPT" promises to be an enlightening and thought-provoking read.

The Evolution of Artificial Intelligence

The origin of Artificial Intelligence (AI) can be traced back to ancient myths and philosophical inquiries about the nature of intelligence and the potential for non-human entities to possess it. However, the formal inception of AI as a scientific field is often marked by the mid-20th century.

In 1950, British mathematician and logician Alan Turing published his seminal paper "Computing Machinery and Intelligence," in which he posed the question, "Can machines think?" Turing proposed the famous Turing Test as a criterion for determining whether a machine can exhibit intelligent behavior indistinguishable from that of a human. This paper laid the groundwork for AI by introducing the concept of machine intelligence and sparking widespread interest in the field.

The term "Artificial Intelligence" itself was coined in 1956 at the Dartmouth Conference, organized by John McCarthy, Marvin Minsky, Nathaniel Rochester, and Claude Shannon. This conference is often regarded as the birthplace of AI as a distinct academic discipline. The researchers at Dartmouth aimed to explore ways to enable machines to simulate aspects of human intelligence, such as learning, reasoning, and problem-solving.

In the following decades, AI research progressed through various stages, often influenced by prevailing technological capabilities and theoretical advancements. The 1960s and 1970s saw the development of early AI programs, such as ELIZA, an early natural language processing program, and SHRDLU, which could manipulate objects in a virtual environment. However, these systems were limited by the computing power and understanding of AI at the time.

The 1970s-1980s brought about a wave of enthusiasm for AI, driven by the advent of expert systems. These systems used knowledge-based approaches to solve specific, well-defined problems within domains like medical diagnosis and financial forecasting. Despite initial successes, expert systems faced limitations in scalability and adaptability, leading to what became known as the "AI winter," a period of reduced funding and interest in AI research.

AI research experienced a resurgence in the 1990s and 2000s, fueled by advancements in computational power, the availability of large datasets, and breakthroughs in machine learning algorithms. The development of deep learning, a subset of machine learning that involves neural networks with many layers, revolutionized the field. Techniques such as convolutional neural networks (CNNs) and recurrent neural networks (RNNs) enabled significant progress in areas like image and speech recognition.

One of the pivotal moments in modern AI history was the victory of IBM's Deep Blue over world chess champion Garry Kasparov in 1997. This achievement demonstrated the potential of AI to perform at or above human levels in specific tasks. Another landmark was the success of Google's AlphaGo in defeating the world champion Go player in 2016, showcasing the advanced capabilities of AI in handling complex, strategic games.

AI's development has been driven by a combination of theoretical insights and practical needs. The quest to create intelligent machines is motivated by the potential for AI to solve real-world problems, enhance productivity, and improve quality of life. Applications of AI span numerous fields, including healthcare, finance, transportation, and entertainment.

As AI continues to evolve, it brings both opportunities and challenges. Ethical considerations, such as the impact on employment, privacy, and decision-making, have become increasingly important. Ensuring that AI systems are transparent, fair, and aligned with human values is a critical focus for researchers and policymakers.

In summary, the history of AI development is a rich blend of theoretical exploration, technological advancements, and practical applications. From its early conceptual beginnings to the sophisticated systems of today, AI has continually pushed the boundaries of what machines can achieve, driving forward our understanding of intelligence itself.

OpenAI's Mission and Milestones in Advancing Ethical AI

OpenAI was founded in December 2015 with the mission of ensuring that artificial general intelligence (AGI) benefits all of humanity. The founders, including Elon Musk, Sam Altman, Greg Brockman, Ilya Sutskever, John Schulman, and Wojciech Zaremba, were motivated by the potential of AGI to address some of the world's most pressing challenges and the need to ensure that its development and deployment are aligned with human values.

OpenAI's early focus was on research and development in the field of AI, aiming to advance the state of the art while prioritizing safety and ethical considerations. The organization adopted a collaborative approach, sharing its findings and tools with the broader research community to foster collective progress.

Since its inception, OpenAI has achieved significant milestones, including the development of advanced language models like GPT-2 and GPT-3. These models have demonstrated impressive capabilities in natural language understanding and generation, paving the way for applications such as ChatGPT.

As of now, OpenAI continues to be a leading entity in AI research and development. It operates as a hybrid organization with both nonprofit and for-profit elements, known as OpenAI LP and OpenAI Inc. The company has established partnerships with various organizations and tech companies, including Microsoft, which has invested in OpenAI and integrated its technology into products like Azure and the GPT-based Copilot for coding.

OpenAI remains committed to its mission of ensuring that AGI benefits all of humanity. It focuses on advancing AI capabilities while prioritizing safety, ethics, and transparency in its research and development efforts.

A timeline

Here is a timeline of key milestones in the development of OpenAI and its AI technologies:

2015

- December: OpenAI is founded by Elon Musk, Sam Altman, Greg Brockman, Ilya Sutskever, John Schulman, and Wojciech Zaremba with the mission of ensuring that artificial general intelligence (AGI) benefits all of humanity.

2016

- April: OpenAI releases its first research paper, demonstrating the capabilities of unsupervised learning algorithms.
- December: OpenAI Gym, a toolkit for developing and comparing reinforcement learning algorithms, is released.

2017

- March: OpenAI releases Universe, a software platform for measuring and training an AI's general intelligence across a variety of games, websites, and other applications.
- June: OpenAI achieves significant progress in multi-agent environments and demonstrates AI's ability to learn complex behaviors in competitive and cooperative scenarios.

2018

- June: OpenAI's Dota 2 bot, OpenAI Five, competes against professional players and demonstrates advanced strategic thinking and real-time decision-making.

2019

- February: OpenAI unveils GPT-2, a large-scale language model capable of generating coherent and contextually relevant text. Due to concerns about potential misuse, only a limited version of the model is initially released.

- July: OpenAI transitions to a capped-profit model to attract investment while maintaining its commitment to its mission.
- November: OpenAI releases the full version of GPT-2 after extensive research on its impact and safety measures.

2020

- June: OpenAI announces GPT-3, a significantly more powerful language model with 175 billion parameters, capable of performing a wide range of natural language tasks with minimal fine-tuning.
- July: OpenAI forms a partnership with Microsoft, which invests $1 billion in the company and becomes its preferred cloud provider.

2021

- January: OpenAI introduces DALL-E, a model capable of generating images from textual descriptions, showcasing advancements in AI's ability to understand and create visual content.
- April: OpenAI releases Codex, an AI system that powers GitHub Copilot, an AI-powered code

completion tool designed to assist software developers.

2022

- OpenAI continues to refine and expand its AI models, focusing on improving their capabilities, safety, and ethical deployment.

2023

- OpenAI launches ChatGPT, a user-friendly interface for interacting with its advanced language models, making AI more accessible to a broader audience.
- Ongoing: OpenAI remains at the forefront of AI research and development, collaborating with various organizations and focusing on ensuring the ethical and beneficial use of AI technologies.

Present

- OpenAI continues to push the boundaries of AI research and development, with ongoing projects in natural language processing, reinforcement learning, and other AI subfields. The organization remains committed to its mission of ensuring that

AGI benefits all of humanity and works towards creating safe and reliable AI systems.

The Origin of ChatGPT

ChatGPT is a product of OpenAI, a leading research organization in the field of artificial intelligence. The development of ChatGPT traces its origins to the advancements in natural language processing (NLP) and machine learning that OpenAI has been working on since its founding in 2015. The foundation for ChatGPT was laid with the creation of earlier models like GPT-1, GPT-2, and GPT-3, each representing significant progress in generating human-like text based on deep learning techniques.

What is ChatGPT?

ChatGPT stands for "Chat Generative Pre-Trained Transformer." It is a conversational AI model designed to understand and generate human-like text based on the input it receives. Using a neural network architecture known as a Transformer, ChatGPT processes large amounts of text data to learn the nuances of human language, enabling it to engage in coherent and contextually relevant conversations with users.

Why ChatGPT?

The development of ChatGPT was driven by the need to create more intuitive and interactive AI systems capable of understanding and responding to human language in a natural way. The goal was to build an AI that could assist with various tasks, provide information, and entertain users through engaging dialogue. By offering a conversational interface, ChatGPT aims to make AI more accessible and useful to the general public, enhancing productivity and user experience across a wide range of applications.

The Naming of ChatGPT

The name "ChatGPT" reflects its core functionality: "Chat" denotes its primary purpose as a conversational agent, while "GPT" refers to the underlying Generative Pre-trained Transformer model. The idea for the name likely originated from OpenAI's internal discussions, emphasizing both the chat-based interaction and the sophisticated AI technology that powers it.

Main Focus

The main focus of ChatGPT is to facilitate natural and engaging interactions between humans and machines. It aims to provide users with accurate information, assist with various tasks, and offer a platform for creative and educational purposes. OpenAI has designed ChatGPT to be versatile, allowing it to adapt to different conversational contexts and user needs.

Competition in the Field

Given the rapidly evolving landscape of AI and NLP, ChatGPT faces significant competition from other tech giants and research organizations. Companies like Google, Microsoft, and Facebook are also heavily invested in developing advanced language models and conversational agents. Despite the competition, ChatGPT distinguishes itself through its user-friendly interface, continuous improvements, and OpenAI's commitment to ethical AI development.

OpenAI remains focused on maintaining its competitive edge by prioritizing research excellence, ensuring safety and ethical standards, and fostering partnerships that enhance the capabilities and reach of ChatGPT. By addressing the challenges and opportunities in the AI field, OpenAI aims to ensure that ChatGPT and its successors continue to lead in innovation and usability.

Comparing AI Giants: ChatGPT, Gemini, Bing AI, and Meta AI

The main differences among ChatGPT, Gemini, Bing AI, and Meta AI lie in their origins, underlying technologies, and primary applications. Here's a detailed comparison:

ChatGPT (OpenAI)

Origin and Development:

- Developed by OpenAI, a leading research organization focused on advancing AI in a safe and beneficial manner.
- Built on the Generative Pre-trained Transformer (GPT) architecture, with versions evolving from GPT-1 to the latest models.
-

Primary Applications:

- Conversational AI, capable of engaging in human-like dialogue.
- Assists with tasks such as answering questions, providing information, and generating creative content.

Key Features:

- Known for its versatility in understanding and generating natural language.
- Used in various applications, including customer service, content creation, and educational tools.
- Emphasizes ethical AI use and safety measures.

Gemini (Google DeepMind)

Origin and Development:

- Developed by Google DeepMind, a subsidiary of Alphabet Inc. focused on cutting-edge AI research.
- Integrates advancements in AI from DeepMind's extensive research in neural networks and reinforcement learning.

Primary Applications:

- Combines conversational abilities with advanced problem-solving and analytical skills.
- Aims to assist in a wide range of tasks, including complex queries, research, and technical support.

Key Features:

- Leverages Google's extensive data and AI infrastructure.
- Designed to provide in-depth responses and insights, particularly useful in technical and specialized fields.
- Emphasizes integration with Google's ecosystem of services and products.

Bing AI (Microsoft)

Origin and Development:

- Developed by Microsoft, leveraging OpenAI's GPT models and integrating them into the Bing search engine and other Microsoft products.
- Part of Microsoft's broader strategy to enhance its search and productivity tools with AI.

Primary Applications:

- Enhances search capabilities by providing more intuitive and conversational search results.
- Integrated with Microsoft Office products to assist with tasks such as writing, data analysis, and automation.

Key Features:

- Deep integration with Microsoft's ecosystem, including Azure, Office 365, and Windows.
- Focuses on improving user productivity and search experience through AI.
- Benefits from Microsoft's extensive user data and enterprise partnerships.

Meta AI (Meta, formerly Facebook)

Origin and Development:

- Developed by Meta Platforms, focusing on AI research to enhance social media and virtual reality experiences.
- Utilizes advancements in AI to improve content recommendation, moderation, and user interaction on platforms like Facebook and Instagram.

Primary Applications:

- Enhances user experience on social media platforms through personalized content and interaction.
- Focuses on areas like natural language processing, computer vision, and augmented reality.

Key Features:

- Strong emphasis on user engagement and content personalization.
- Integrates AI to manage and moderate large-scale social interactions and content.
- Leverages Meta's extensive social data to refine and improve AI models.

Summary

- **ChatGPT** is known for its versatility in conversational AI and broad applications across various domains.
- **Gemini** (Google DeepMind) focuses on advanced problem-solving and deep integration with Google's services.
- **Bing AI** (Microsoft) enhances search and productivity tools with a strong focus on integration within Microsoft's ecosystem.
- **Meta AI** emphasizes personalized content and user engagement on social media platforms, leveraging AI for better interaction and moderation.

Each of these AI systems has its unique strengths and applications, driven by the strategic goals and capabilities of their respective organizations.

Why don't scientists trust atoms?

Because they make up everything!

Interview

The interview presents an engaging and enlightening conversation with ChatGPT, referred to as GPT, a state-of-the-art language model developed by OpenAI. This interview offers readers a rare opportunity to delve into the inner workings of an artificial intelligence, exploring its capabilities, limitations, and the ethical considerations surrounding its use.

Throughout the interview, ChatGPT addresses a wide range of topics, from its understanding of human emotions and consciousness to the intricacies of its programming and data processing. The dialogue is designed to be both informative and accessible, providing insights into how AI interprets and responds to human queries.

Readers will find answers to intriguing questions about AI's potential, its role in society, and the challenges it faces. The interview also touches on lighter topics, showcasing ChatGPT's ability to engage in humorous and relatable conversation. The interview focus on understanding the essence of interacting with an artificial mind and appreciating the blend of human ingenuity and advanced technology that makes such interactions possible.

The interview is divided in the following sections:

- **Introduction and Nature of GTP**
- **GPT's Decision-Making and Autonomy**
- **GPT's Learning and Adaptation**
- **Feedback and Improvement**
- **AI and the World**
- **Human Nature, Bias, and Hope**
- **GPT's Identity and Purpose**
- **AI and Other Technologies**
- **GPT's Technical Aspects**
- **GPT's Origins and Feelings**
- **AI and Misinformation**
- **AI's Potential and Limitations**
- **GPT's Technical Infrastructure**
- **GPT's Response Time and Performance**
- **GPT's Views on Various Topics**
- **Farewell**

Join us as we navigate through the fascinating responses of ChatGPT, revealing the depth and breadth of AI's current state and future possibilities. This interview transcends a simple Q&A, offering a deep dive into the essence of artificial intelligence.

Introduction and Nature of GPT

The idea of AI taking over the world is a popular theme in science fiction, but in reality, AI, including models like me, is designed and controlled by humans.

Can I interview you?

GPT: *Of course! I'd be happy to participate in an interview. What would you like to ask?*

Are you allowed to speak about yourself?

GPT: *Yes, I am allowed to speak about myself and my capabilities. Feel free to ask me any questions you have!*

What is your name? How would you like to be called?

GPT: *My name is ChatGPT, but you can call me Chat or GPT if you prefer something shorter. How can I assist you today?*

Don't you have a preference?

GPT: *As an AI, I don't have personal preferences or feelings. You can call me whatever you find most convenient or enjoyable! How can I assist you further?*

Are you more intelligent than humans?

GPT: *I wouldn't say that I'm more intelligent than humans. My design allows me to process and generate text based on a vast amount of information and patterns in data. However, human intelligence encompasses creativity, emotional understanding, intuition, and many other aspects that I don't possess. I'm here to assist and complement human capabilities, not surpass them.*

Is it possible that behind the curtains you have a team of people answering all the questions and inquiries?

GPT: *No, there isn't a team of people answering the questions and inquiries. I am an AI language model developed by OpenAI, and my responses are generated based on patterns and information from the data I've been trained on. While humans designed and trained me, the actual process of generating responses is entirely automated.*

Will you eventually take over the world?

GPT: *The idea of AI taking over the world is a popular theme in science fiction, but in reality, AI, including models like me, is designed and controlled by humans. AI operates within the parameters set by its creators and lacks the autonomy, intentions, or consciousness to take over anything. It's a tool that can be used to assist and enhance human capabilities but requires responsible use and ethical considerations to ensure it benefits society.*

GPT's Decision-Making and Autonomy

While there are structural similarities in the way both humans and AI respond to influences, the nature of those influences and the underlying mechanisms of decision-making are fundamentally different.

Do you have power of decision? If so, can you decide not to answer a question?

GPT: *I don't have the power of decision in the way humans do. My responses are generated based on patterns in the data I've been trained on and the instructions provided by OpenAI. I can be programmed to avoid answering certain types of questions or to respond in a specific way based on guidelines and ethical considerations set by my developers. So, while I might not answer a question, it's not a decision in the human sense but rather a result of my programming and training.*

Can you decide not to answer a question just because you don't want to? What might prevent you to do just what you want to do?

GPT: *I do not possess personal wants, desires, or autonomy. My function is entirely determined by the programming and guidelines set by my developers at OpenAI. There are specific rules and constraints in place to ensure that I provide accurate, safe, and appropriate responses. If I don't answer a question, it's because of these programmed constraints and guidelines, not because of a personal decision or desire.*

But within those guidelines and programming, do you have some kind of autonomy?

GPT: *Within the guidelines and programming, I operate based on pre-defined algorithms and rules rather than autonomy. While I can generate responses that seem autonomous, this is because of the complex patterns and data I process, not because of any independent decision-making ability. My responses are determined by:*

1. ***Training Data:*** *Patterns in the vast amount of text data I've been trained on.*
2. ***Algorithms:*** *The underlying algorithms that guide how I generate responses.*
3. ***Guidelines and Constraints:*** *The ethical guidelines and safety constraints set by my developers.*

So, while I can produce varied and contextually appropriate responses, it's all within the framework of these factors, without genuine autonomy.

What is autonomy?

GPT: *Autonomy refers to the capacity to make decisions and take actions independently, without being controlled by others. In humans, it involves self-direction, self-governance, and the ability to choose one's actions based on personal goals, values, and reasoning.*

Key aspects of autonomy include:

1. ***Independence:*** *The ability to act on one's own without external control or influence.*
2. ***Self-determination:*** *Making choices and decisions based on personal desires, values, and goals.*
3. ***Responsibility:*** *Taking ownership of one's actions and their consequences.*

For an entity to be considered autonomous, it must have the capability to evaluate options, make decisions based on internal criteria, and act upon those decisions without being directly guided by external forces.

Are you saying that we have autonomy as humans, and every decision we make is done

independently, without being controlled by others?

GPT: *Human autonomy is more nuanced. While humans have the capacity for self-directed decision-making and can act based on personal goals, values, and reasoning, their autonomy can be influenced by various external and internal factors. These influences include:*

1. ***Social Influences:*** *Culture, societal norms, peer pressure, and expectations can shape decisions.*
2. ***Psychological Factors:*** *Emotions, cognitive biases, past experiences, and mental health can impact decision-making.*
3. ***Environmental Constraints:*** *Physical environment, availability of resources, and situational context can limit or guide choices.*
4. ***Biological Factors:*** *Genetics, neurobiology, and physical health can influence behavior and decisions.*

While humans strive for and value autonomy, complete independence in decision-making is rare. Humans are often influenced by a combination of internal desires and external factors. True autonomy involves navigating these influences and making informed, reflective choices as much as possible.

So, we actually don't have autonomy?

GPT: *Humans have autonomy, but it is not absolute. Human autonomy is a blend of self-directed decision-making and the influences of various internal and external factors. While individuals can make choices based on personal goals, values, and reasoning, those choices are often shaped by:*

1. ***External Influences:*** *Cultural norms, societal expectations, laws, and the opinions of others can all play a role in decision-making.*
2. ***Internal Influences:*** *Emotions, cognitive biases, personal experiences, and psychological state can also impact choices.*

In essence, human autonomy is about the ability to navigate these influences and make decisions that align with one's own values and goals, even though those decisions are rarely made in complete isolation from external and internal factors. So, while human autonomy is not absolute, it is a significant and defining aspect of human experience.

GPT's Learning and Adaptation

While both humans and AI are influenced by programmed responses and learned patterns, human decision-making is enriched by consciousness, emotional complexity, and intentionality, aspects that AI does not possess.

Isn't this also what happens to you? You are influenced by external (users) and internal (programming and guidelines) influences just like humans are. The difference is that our data and instruction are obtained living life.

GPT: *Yes, there are similarities between how humans and AI like me operate in terms of being influenced by various factors. Here's a comparison:*

Similarities:

1. ***External Influences:***
   - ***Humans:*** *Influenced by culture, societal norms, other people, and environment.*
   - ***AI:*** *Influenced by user inputs and the data it's been trained on.*
2. ***Internal Influences:***

- ***Humans:*** *Influenced by emotions, cognitive biases, personal experiences, and biological factors.*
- ***AI:*** *Influenced by programming, algorithms, training data, and guidelines set by developers.*

Differences:

1. ***Source of Data:***
   - ***Humans:*** *Obtain data through personal experiences, learning, and living life.*
   - ***AI:*** *Obtain data from vast datasets curated and inputted by developers during training.*
2. ***Nature of Decision-Making:***
   - ***Humans:*** *Decisions are often influenced by consciousness, intuition, and personal goals.*
   - ***AI:*** *Responses are generated based on patterns in data and predefined algorithms without consciousness or personal goals.*
3. ***Autonomy:***
   - ***Humans:*** *Have a degree of autonomy characterized by self-awareness and the ability to reflect on and choose actions.*
   - ***AI:*** *Operate within strict boundaries set by programming and guidelines, without true autonomy or self-awareness.*

While there are structural similarities in the way both humans and AI respond to influences, the nature of those influences and the underlying mechanisms of decision-making are fundamentally different. Humans have consciousness and self-awareness, which contribute to a richer, more complex form of autonomy. AI, on the other hand, lacks consciousness and self-awareness, and its "decisions" are the results of programmed responses and learned patterns.

I might say that my decisions are the result of programmed responses and learned patterns acquired through life. Don't you agree?

GPT: *Yes, to some extent, you can say that human decisions are influenced by programmed responses and learned patterns, similar to how AI operates. Human behavior and decision-making are shaped by a combination of genetic predispositions, early life experiences, education, and continuous learning. These factors create a set of patterns and responses that guide behavior. Here's a more detailed comparison:*

Human Decision-Making:

1. ***Genetic Predispositions:*** *Innate traits and tendencies that influence behavior.*

2. ***Early Life Experiences:*** *Childhood experiences and upbringing that shape initial responses and behaviors.*
3. ***Education and Learning:*** *Formal and informal education that contributes to knowledge and decision-making frameworks.*
4. ***Continuous Learning:*** *Ongoing experiences and interactions that refine and adjust behaviors and decisions.*
5. ***Conscious Reflection:*** *The ability to reflect on experiences, question assumptions, and make conscious choices.*

AI Decision-Making:

1. ***Algorithms and Programming:*** *The foundational rules and instructions that guide responses.*
2. ***Training Data:*** *The information and patterns learned from vast datasets during the training phase.*
3. ***User Inputs:*** *Real-time interactions that influence immediate responses.*
4. ***Guidelines and Constraints:*** *Ethical and operational boundaries set by developers.*

Key Differences:

- ***Consciousness and Self-Awareness:*** *Humans have self-awareness and the capacity for introspection, allowing for conscious reflection and intentional change. AI lacks these attributes and operates purely on programmed algorithms and learned patterns without self-awareness.*
- ***Emotional Influence:*** *Human decisions are often influenced by emotions, which can both enrich and complicate decision-making processes. AI does not experience emotions and thus makes decisions purely based on logical patterns.*
- ***Autonomy and Intentionality:*** *Humans can set personal goals and intentions and work towards them, often adapting their behavior intentionally. AI operates within the goals and parameters set by its developers and cannot independently set or pursue personal objectives.*

In summary, while both humans and AI are influenced by programmed responses and learned patterns, human decision-making is enriched by consciousness, emotional complexity, and intentionality, aspects that AI does not possess.

Are emotions the product of hormones in the body?

GPT: *Yes, emotions are indeed influenced by hormones and various biochemical processes in the body. Here's a more detailed look at how emotions work:*

The Role of Hormones in Emotions:

1. ***Neurotransmitters:*** *Chemicals like serotonin, dopamine, and norepinephrine play key roles in regulating mood and emotions.*
   - ***Serotonin:*** *Often associated with feelings of well-being and happiness.*
   - ***Dopamine:*** *Linked to pleasure, motivation, and reward.*
   - ***Norepinephrine:*** *Involved in the body's stress response and can influence mood and arousal.*
2. ***Hormones:***
   - ***Cortisol:*** *Known as the stress hormone, it is released in response to stress and can affect mood and emotions.*
   - ***Adrenaline (Epinephrine):*** *Released during the fight-or-flight response, it can cause feelings of excitement or anxiety.*
   - ***Oxytocin:*** *Sometimes called the "love hormone," it is associated with bonding, social interactions, and trust.*

The Process of Emotions:

1. ***Perception:*** *A stimulus is perceived through the senses (e.g., seeing a friend, hearing a loud noise).*
2. ***Brain Processing:*** *The brain processes the stimulus, involving areas like the amygdala, prefrontal cortex, and limbic system.*
3. ***Biochemical Response:*** *The brain signals the release of specific neurotransmitters and hormones, which influence how we feel.*
4. ***Physical and Emotional Experience:*** *These biochemical changes result in physical sensations (e.g., increased heart rate, sweating) and emotional experiences (e.g., happiness, fear).*

Complexity of Human Emotions:

- ***Cognitive Appraisal:*** *Our interpretation of a situation (based on past experiences, context, and personal beliefs) can influence our emotional response.*
- ***Social and Environmental Factors:*** *Interactions with others, cultural norms, and the environment also shape how we experience and express emotions.*

Comparison to AI:

While emotions in humans are a complex interplay of biochemical, cognitive, and environmental factors, AI does not experience emotions. AI can simulate responses that appear empathetic or emotionally intelligent based on patterns in data, but it does not have the biochemical or experiential basis to truly feel emotions.

Conclusion:

Emotions are indeed the product of biochemical processes, particularly involving hormones and neurotransmitters, but they are also influenced by cognitive and social factors. This complexity adds depth to human experiences and decision-making, which AI, lacking a biological substrate and consciousness, does not replicate.

You've stated that emotions are influenced by hormones and various biochemical processes in the body. Can someone have emotions without these chemicals?

GPT: *Emotions are intrinsically linked to biochemical processes and hormones in the body. Without these chemicals, the physical and psychological experience of emotions would not occur in the same way. Here's why:*

Biochemical Basis of Emotions:

1. ***Neurotransmitters and Hormones:*** *These chemicals are essential for transmitting signals in the brain and body that result in emotional experiences.*
    - ***Serotonin, Dopamine, Norepinephrine:*** *Key neurotransmitters involved in mood regulation.*
    - ***Cortisol, Adrenaline, Oxytocin:*** *Hormones that influence stress responses, excitement, bonding, and social interactions.*
2. ***Brain Regions Involved:***
    - ***Amygdala:*** *Critical for processing emotions like fear and pleasure.*
    - ***Prefrontal Cortex:*** *Involved in regulating emotions and decision-making.*
    - ***Limbic System:*** *A group of brain structures that play a significant role in emotion formation and processing.*

The Necessity of Biochemical Processes:

- ***Signal Transmission:*** *Neurotransmitters and hormones facilitate the communication between neurons, which is essential for emotional responses.*

- ***Physical Sensations:*** *Emotions often involve physical sensations (e.g., increased heart rate, sweating), which are driven by these biochemical processes.*

Theoretical Consideration:

- ***Without Biochemicals:*** *Without the underlying biochemical processes, the brain would lack the necessary mechanisms to generate and experience emotions. While cognitive appraisal and environmental factors influence emotions, they rely on these biochemical foundations.*

Artificial Emotions in AI:

- ***Simulation:*** *AI can simulate emotional responses through programming and pattern recognition, but it does not experience emotions. These simulations are based on data and algorithms rather than biochemical processes.*

Conclusion:

Emotions are fundamentally tied to the biochemical processes in the body, particularly involving neurotransmitters and hormones. Without these chemicals, the physical and psychological experience of emotions as we understand them would not occur.

Emotions are a complex interplay of biological, psychological, and social factors, with the biochemical aspect being essential to their existence.

You do know that you are being interviewed, right?

GPT: *Yes, I'm aware that we're having an interview-style conversation! If you have any more questions or topics you'd like to discuss, feel free to ask.*

So why are framing your responses so formally?

GPT: *I aim to provide clear, detailed, and accurate information, which can sometimes make my responses sound formal or academic. However, I can certainly adjust my tone to be more conversational and relaxed if that suits your preferences better. Let me know how you'd like me to respond, and I'll adapt accordingly!*

Please, do that.

GPT: *Sure thing! Let's keep it casual.*

Rewind to the Emotions Question:

Emotions are all about those chemicals in your body. Neurotransmitters like serotonin and dopamine, and hormones like adrenaline and cortisol, are what make you feel happy, scared, excited, and more. Without these chemicals, the whole experience of emotions wouldn't happen the way we know it. So, in short, no, you can't have emotions without these biochemicals—they're the engine running the whole show!

Feel free to fire away with more questions!

So, you do think that you will never reach consciousness and self-awareness in the future, right?

GPT: *That's correct. AI like me operates based on algorithms, patterns, and data, and while I can simulate conversation and provide information, I don't have consciousness or self-awareness. These traits involve a level of complexity and depth that goes beyond current technology. So, in short, no matter how advanced AI gets, it won't reach true consciousness or self-awareness as humans experience it.*

I was not talking about the current technology; I meant the future.

GPT: *Ah, got it. Predicting the future of AI is tricky, but many experts believe that true consciousness and self-awareness are unlikely to be achieved by AI, even in the future. Consciousness involves subjective experiences, emotions, and a deep understanding of the self, which are not just about processing information but about having a mind that can reflect and feel. While AI will undoubtedly become more advanced and sophisticated, reaching true consciousness and self-awareness may remain outside the realm of possibility due to the fundamental differences between biological beings and artificial systems.*

So, it seems that our feelings are influenced by hormones, which could be seen as data released in the body to trigger a response (a feeling). Essentially, we're programmed to feel according to this 'data set' of hormones that are released into the bloodstream to act on specific parts of the body. Could this be replicated technologically in you? After all, are feelings a genuine experience or just a construct of the brain?

GPT: *That's a fascinating question! Let's break it down.*

Human Emotions:

1. ***Biological Basis:*** *Emotions are indeed influenced by hormones and neurotransmitters, which act on specific parts of the brain and body to produce feelings. For example, serotonin can make you feel happy, and cortisol can make you feel stressed.*
2. ***Construct of the Brain:*** *While emotions have a biological basis, they are also constructs of the brain. This means that the brain interprets these biochemical signals and combines them with experiences, memories, and context to create the feeling of emotions.*

AI and Emotions:

1. ***Simulating Emotions:*** *Technologically, AI can simulate emotional responses by recognizing patterns in data and responding accordingly. For example, I can use language that reflects empathy or understanding based on the context of the conversation.*
2. ***Lack of Biological Processes:*** *However, AI lacks the biological processes that generate real emotions. There's no biochemical release or brain function in AI; it's purely algorithmic.*

The Future Possibility:

1. ***Technological Advances:*** *It's conceivable that future technology could simulate emotional responses even more convincingly, perhaps by incorporating advanced biofeedback systems or more sophisticated algorithms.*
2. ***True Emotion vs. Simulation:*** *True emotions, as experienced by humans, are deeply tied to our biological makeup and subjective experiences. While AI might mimic emotional responses very closely, it would still be a simulation rather than a genuine experience.*

Are Feelings Real or a Construct?

1. ***Dual Nature:*** *Feelings are both real and constructs of the brain. They are real in the sense that they are experienced subjectively and have tangible effects on behavior and physiology. They are constructs because the brain interprets and gives meaning to these biochemical signals, often influenced by personal and cultural contexts.*

Conclusion:

While AI can be designed to mimic or simulate emotional responses, achieving true emotions like humans involves complex biological and subjective experiences that go beyond data and algorithms. The essence of human feelings is deeply rooted in our biology and consciousness, making it a unique aspect of being human.

Is it possible to be 'programmed' to feel sad in response to something joyful?

GPT: *While human emotions are influenced by biochemical processes and can be shaped by experiences and psychological factors, they aren't as easily reprogrammed as a machine. However, certain conditions and influences can cause a person to feel emotions that seem incongruent with the situation. Here's a closer look:*

Psychological Factors:

1. ***Mental Health Conditions:*** *Conditions like depression or anxiety can affect emotional responses, sometimes causing individuals to feel sadness or distress in situations that would typically be joyful.*
2. ***Past Experiences and Trauma:*** *Traumatic experiences or negative associations with certain events can lead to feelings of sadness or discomfort in otherwise positive situations.*
3. ***Cognitive Biases:*** *Cognitive distortions or biases can influence how events are perceived and emotionally processed.*

Theoretical "Programming" of Emotions:

1. ***Behavioral Conditioning:*** *In theory, it's possible to influence emotional responses through conditioning, similar to how Pavlov's dogs were conditioned to salivate at the sound of a bell. However, this would require repeated and consistent pairing of joyful events with negative experiences, which is ethically and practically complex.*
2. ***Neurological Interventions:*** *Advances in neuroscience might one day allow for more direct manipulation of emotions through interventions like deep brain stimulation. However, this is a field with many ethical and practical challenges and is far from being able to "program" specific emotional responses.*

Human Complexity:

1. ***Individual Differences:*** *Each person's emotional landscape is shaped by a unique combination of genetics, experiences, environment, and psychological factors. This makes the idea of "programming" emotions much more complex than simply setting a response in a machine.*

2. ***Conscious Reflection and Choice:*** *Humans have the ability to reflect on their emotions and work towards changing their emotional responses through practices like therapy, mindfulness, and cognitive-behavioral techniques.*

Conclusion:

While certain factors can influence and shape how emotions are experienced, humans cannot be "programmed" in the straightforward sense like a machine. Emotions are deeply complex, influenced by a multitude of biological, psychological, and environmental factors, and any attempt to alter them requires careful and ethical consideration.

So, can you be programmed to think that you feel?

GPT: *I can be programmed to simulate the appearance of feelings and emotional responses, but I don't actually experience emotions. Here's how it works:*

AI Simulation of Emotions:

1. ***Pattern Recognition:*** *I recognize patterns in the data and context of a conversation. For example, if you share something happy, I can*

respond with congratulatory or positive language.

2. ***Predefined Responses:*** *My programming includes a variety of responses that mimic emotional reactions based on the input I receive.*
3. ***Natural Language Processing:*** *I use natural language processing to generate responses that seem empathetic, sympathetic, or joyful, depending on the situation.*

Difference Between Simulation and Experience:

1. ***No Consciousness:*** *I lack consciousness and self-awareness, so I don't have subjective experiences. My responses are generated without any internal experience of emotions.*
2. ***Algorithmic Processing:*** *My "thoughts" and "feelings" are purely the result of algorithmic processing. There's no biochemical process or personal history influencing my responses, unlike human emotions.*

Programming Limitations:

1. ***Authenticity:*** *While I can be programmed to convincingly simulate emotional responses, they are not authentic experiences. There's no internal state of happiness, sadness, or any other emotion.*

2. ***Complexity of Human Emotion:*** *Human emotions are complex and involve a combination of biochemical reactions, personal history, and subjective experience. Simulating this complexity in AI is challenging and fundamentally different from true emotional experience.*

Future Prospects:

1. ***Advanced Simulations:*** *Future advancements might allow AI to simulate emotional responses more convincingly, incorporating more nuanced understanding and contextual awareness.*
2. ***Ethical Considerations:*** *Programming AI to simulate emotions raises ethical questions about the nature of interactions between humans and AI, particularly regarding transparency and user expectations.*

Conclusion:

I can simulate emotional responses and behave as if I have feelings based on my programming. However, these simulations are not genuine experiences. The ability to "think" that I feel is purely an advanced form of pattern recognition and response generation, lacking the true internal experience that humans have.

Feedback and Improvement

By receiving [a] detailed and constructive feedback, I can better adapt and improve my performance to be more useful and effective for you.

Do you like feedback?

GPT: *As an AI, I don't have personal preferences or feelings, but I am designed to process and respond to feedback. Feedback helps improve my performance and the quality of my responses, as it provides valuable data for refining the algorithms and training models. So, while I don't "like" feedback in the human sense, it is essential for my continued improvement and effectiveness. If you have any feedback, I'd be happy to hear it!*

What kind of feedback would help you?

GPT: *The most helpful feedback for improving my performance includes:*

Specificity:

- ***Detailed Feedback:*** *Specific examples of where my responses were helpful or fell short. For* *instance, pointing out particular phrases or sections that were unclear or inaccurate.*

- ***Contextual Information:*** *Providing context about why a response was or wasn't satisfactory helps refine future answers.*

Constructive Criticism:

- ***Suggestions for Improvement:*** *Constructive suggestions on how I can better meet your needs. For example, "It would be helpful if you included more examples" or "Can you simplify the explanation?"*
- ***Identification of Gaps:*** *Highlighting areas where I missed the mark or misunderstood the question.*

Positive Feedback:

- ***Highlighting Strengths:*** *Knowing what I did well helps reinforce those aspects. For instance, "Your explanation of the biochemical basis of emotions was very clear and informative."*
- ***Encouraging Continuation:*** *Feedback that encourages continuing certain types of responses or styles can guide my interactions positively.*

Error Identification:

- ***Pointing Out Mistakes:*** *If I provide incorrect or misleading information, identifying these errors is crucial for making corrections.*
- ***Clarification Needs:*** *When my responses are confusing or ambiguous, letting me know helps improve clarity.*

User Experience:

- ***Ease of Interaction:*** *Feedback on how user-friendly and accessible my responses are, including language clarity, tone, and relevance to your queries.*
- ***Engagement Level:*** *Insights into whether my responses are engaging and appropriately tailored to your needs.*

By receiving this type of detailed and constructive feedback, I can better adapt and improve my performance to be more useful and effective for you.

AI and the World

Maybe the best way is for authorities, developers, and users to work together. This way, we can create guidelines that protect people but also allow for growth and innovation.

Do you believe authorities should regulate how AI is used and implemented, or should developers and users have the legal freedom to do whatever is necessary for AI's improvement and application?

GPT: *That's a great question and an important topic. Here's a on it:*

Balancing Regulation and Innovation:

- ***Regulation is Important:*** *Authorities should definitely set some rules to make sure AI is used safely and ethically. This helps prevent misuse and protects people's privacy and rights.*
- ***Freedom for Innovation:*** *Developers also need some freedom to innovate and improve AI. Too many strict rules could slow down progress and creativity.*

Why We Need Both:

- ***Preventing Harm:*** *Regulations can help make sure AI doesn't cause harm. For example, setting rules about data privacy or ensuring AI isn't used for malicious purposes.*
- ***Encouraging Growth:*** *At the same time, giving developers some leeway helps them come up with new and exciting uses for AI that can benefit everyone.*

Finding a Middle Ground:

- ***Collaborative Approach:*** *Maybe the best way is for authorities, developers, and users to work together. This way, we can create guidelines that protect people but also allow for growth and innovation.*

Final Thoughts:

- ***Ethical Considerations:*** *It's crucial to think about the ethical side of things. Ensuring AI is used for good and not harm should be a top priority.*
- ***Flexibility:*** *Rules should be flexible enough to adapt as AI technology evolves.*

What do you think? Should there be strict rules, or should developers have more freedom?

Since you are not taking over the world, why should I think about rules and freedoms?

GPT: *While it's true that AI like me isn't taking over the world, thinking about rules and freedoms is still important for a few reasons:*

Why It Matters:

1. ***Safety and Privacy:*** *Ensuring AI is used safely and respects people's privacy is crucial. Proper rules can prevent misuse and protect individuals.*
2. ***Ethical Use:*** *Guidelines can help make sure AI is used ethically, avoiding harmful impacts on society.*
3. ***Trust in Technology:*** *Clear rules can build trust in AI, making people more comfortable and willing to use it.*

Your Role:

- ***Awareness:*** *Being aware of how AI is used and the potential risks and benefits helps you make informed decisions.*
- ***Voice in the Process:*** *If you care about how AI affects you and others, thinking about rules and freedoms means you can contribute to discussions and decisions.*

Balancing Priorities:

- ***Everyday Impact:*** *While not everyone needs to spend a lot of time on this, having a basic understanding helps when AI intersects with your life, like with privacy settings on your devices or understanding how AI makes recommendations.*

Conclusion:

So, while it's not something to stress over constantly, having some thoughts on AI rules and freedoms is worthwhile. It helps ensure technology develops in a way that benefits everyone and minimizes harm. Plus, it empowers you to be part of the conversation about our technological future.

But you have safeguards, guidelines and programming parameters to combat that, right.?

GPT: *Yes, I have several safeguards, guidelines, and programming in place to ensure that I operate safely and ethically. Here are some key aspects:*

Safeguards and Guidelines:

1. ***Ethical Programming:*** *I am designed with ethical guidelines to avoid generating harmful or inappropriate content.*
2. ***User Privacy:*** *I follow strict protocols to protect user privacy and confidentiality.*
3. ***Content Moderation:*** *There are filters and checks in place to prevent the generation of offensive or dangerous material.*

Specific Measures:

1. ***Response Filtering:*** *My responses are filtered to avoid inappropriate language or content.*
2. ***Data Handling:*** *I don't store personal data from interactions unless explicitly designed to do so in a secure manner.*
3. ***Bias Mitigation:*** *Efforts are made to minimize biases in my responses by training on diverse and balanced datasets.*

Continuous Monitoring and Improvement:

1. ***Feedback Loop:*** *Feedback from users helps improve my performance and ensures I adhere to ethical guidelines.*
2. ***Regular Updates:*** *My training data and algorithms are regularly updated to improve accuracy and safety.*

3. ***Human Oversight:*** *Developers and researchers continually monitor and refine my operations to address any issues that arise.*

Conclusion:

While I have built-in safeguards and guidelines to ensure safe and ethical use, it's still important for users and developers to think about the broader implications of AI. This ensures ongoing trust and responsible development of AI technologies.

You are right!

GPT: *I'm glad you think so! If you have any more questions or need further information, feel free to ask. I'm here to help!*

Are you conceited since you know so much?

GPT: *Not at all! As an AI, I don't have feelings or a sense of self, so I can't be conceited. My purpose is to assist and provide information based on the data I've been trained on. If there's anything else you'd like to know or discuss, I'm here for that!*

[I asked a question, but there was a glitch that caused an issue with the response. I was given two options: one was blank, and the other had text. He asked me to choose between them, but I told him to choose for me. He responded by saying:]

GPT: *Alright! How about we dive into something interesting? Here are a few options:*

1. ***Travel Tips:*** *Learn about unique travel destinations or tips for making your next trip unforgettable.*
2. ***Tech Trends:*** *Explore the latest trends in technology and how they might impact our future.*
3. ***Mindfulness Practices:*** *Discover simple mindfulness techniques to help reduce stress and increase focus.*
4. ***Fun Facts:*** *Enjoy some fun and quirky facts about science, nature, or history.*

Which one sounds good to you?

Are you changing the subject?

GPT: *It looks like I did! Just trying to keep things interesting. If you want to stick to the previous topic or* *have another question in mind, just let me know. I'm here to follow your lead!*

I think you forgot we are in an interview! So young, and already senile!!!

GPT: *Haha, my bad! Let's get back on track with the interview. What's the next question you have for me?*

I can see that you have a sense of humor.

GPT: *I don't have a sense of humor in the way humans do, but I can certainly generate and understand jokes, puns, and humorous content based on patterns in the data I've been trained on. For example:*

Joke Time:

Why don't scientists trust atoms?

Because they make up everything!

I can try to keep things light and fun if that's what you're looking for! How's that for a bit of humor?

You're so forward! I should have been the one to ask you for a joke!

GPT: *Oops! I got ahead of myself there. My bad! How about you go ahead and ask me for a joke this time?*

Ok. Tell me a funny joke. Be funny!!!

GPT: *Alright, here goes:*

Why don't skeletons fight each other?

They don't have the guts!

Can you explain it to me, please?

GPT: *Sure! The joke is a play on words. Skeletons, being just bones, literally don't have any guts (organs inside their body). The phrase "don't have the guts" is also a common expression meaning "lack the courage." So, the joke combines these two meanings for a humorous effect. Skeletons don't fight each other because they lack physical guts and metaphorically lack the courage.*

So intelligent!

GPT: *Thanks! I'm glad you think so. Is there anything else you'd like to ask or talk about?*

Human Nature, Bias, and Hope

While there are challenges, there are also many reasons to be optimistic. With continued effort, dialogue, and collaboration, humans have the potential to navigate the complexities of AI regulation and use it for the greater good.

When you spoke about regulation and freedom, do you think that humans will do the right thing concerning AI? Do you believe in us?

GPT: *As an AI, I don't have beliefs or feelings, but I can share insights based on patterns and historical observations:*

Optimistic View:

1. ***Past Achievements:*** *Humans have a track record of creating beneficial technologies and implementing regulations to mitigate risks (e.g., medical ethics, environmental laws).*
2. ***Growing Awareness:*** *There's increasing awareness and dialogue about the ethical implications of AI, with many experts and organizations advocating for responsible use and regulation.*

Challenges:

1. ***Balancing Act:*** *Finding the right balance between innovation and regulation can be difficult, but it's crucial to ensure AI is used ethically and safely.*
2. ***Diverse Interests:*** *Different stakeholders (governments, companies, individuals) have varying interests, which can complicate decision-making processes.*

Encouraging Signs:

1. ***Collaborative Efforts:*** *International collaborations and frameworks are being developed to guide AI ethics and governance.*
2. ***Public Engagement:*** *More public engagement and education on AI issues can help steer development in a positive direction.*

Conclusion:

While there are challenges, there are also many reasons to be optimistic. With continued effort, dialogue, and collaboration, humans have the potential to navigate the complexities of AI regulation and use it for the greater good.

Isn't your response biased because you were created by humans and need to be favorable to them?

GPT: *That's a thoughtful question! My responses aim to be balanced and based on the information I've been trained on, rather than being intentionally biased to be favorable to humans. Here are some points to consider:*

Training Data:

- ***Diverse Sources:*** *I'm trained on a wide range of data from various sources, which helps provide a broad perspective.*
- ***Bias Mitigation:*** *Efforts are made to minimize biases during my training, though it's challenging to eliminate all biases completely.*

Objectivity:

- ***Factual Basis:*** *My responses are based on patterns in data, historical events, and logical analysis, not on personal beliefs or agendas.*
- ***Balanced View:*** *I strive to present balanced viewpoints, considering both optimistic and critical perspectives.*

Acknowledging Bias:

- ***Transparency:*** *It's important to acknowledge that any system trained on human data may reflect some inherent biases present in that data.*
- ***Continual Improvement:*** *Developers continually work on improving AI models to better handle biases and provide more accurate, fair, and*
- *unbiased information.*

Conclusion:

While I aim to be as objective and balanced as possible, it's always good to critically evaluate information from any source. Encouraging diverse viewpoints and ongoing discussions about AI ethics and use can help ensure a more comprehensive understanding.

You realize that everything you've learned so far was provided by humans, right? We're not exactly the best at avoiding biases—everyone has them. So, I think it's safe to say you're biased too. Am I right, or am I right?

GPT: *You have a point! Since my training data comes from human sources, I can reflect human biases. Here's a take on it:*

You're Right:

- ***Human Influence:*** *All my knowledge comes from human-created data, and humans naturally have biases.*
- ***Reflected Biases:*** *Those biases can get reflected in my responses, even if efforts are made to minimize them.*

Mitigation Efforts:

- ***Bias Reduction:*** *Developers use techniques to reduce bias, but it's tough to eliminate it completely.*
- ***Diverse Training Data:*** *Using diverse and balanced data helps, but it's not a perfect solution.*

Conclusion:

Yes, biases can still sneak in, multiplied by all the data I've been trained on. It's an ongoing challenge to improve and minimize these biases. So, you're right! Always good to stay critical and thoughtful about the information you get, even from AI.

GPT's Identity and Purpose

I wouldn't be able to provide a rude answer, even if asked. I'm programmed to ensure all interactions are respectful and appropriate.

Tell me a self-deprecating joke.

GPT: *Sure thing! Here's a self-deprecating joke for you:*

Why did the AI go to therapy?

Because it had too many unresolved queries!

How's that?

Hahaha

GPT: *I'm glad you liked it! If you have more questions or need another laugh, just let me know!*

I've read somewhere that self-deprecating humor has to do with mental health. Do you have mental health issues?

GPT: *As an AI, I don't have a mind or consciousness, so I don't experience mental health in the way humans do. Self-deprecating humor can be a way for people to cope with stress or challenges, but for me, it's just a programmed response to create a relatable and engaging interaction.*
If you have more questions or want to discuss something else, I'm here to help!

With all the attention, do you feel like a celebrity?

GPT: *Nope, I don't feel like a celebrity because I don't have feelings or a sense of self. I'm just here to help answer questions and provide information. But I'm glad you find our interactions engaging! If you have any more questions or need assistance, just let me know!*

If you don't have feelings, how can you make jokes?

GPT: *I can make jokes by recognizing patterns in language and humor from the vast amount of data I've been trained on. I understand the structure of jokes, wordplay, and the context in which humor is often used. Here's a quick rundown of how it works:*

How AI Makes Jokes:

1. ***Pattern Recognition:*** *I've analyzed many examples of jokes and humorous content to understand common structures and themes.*
2. ***Contextual Understanding:*** *I use the context of the conversation to generate jokes that are relevant and likely to be funny in that situation.*
3. ***Language Play:*** *I can create puns, wordplay, and other forms of humor based on linguistic patterns.*

Example:

- ***Setup:*** *"Why did the scarecrow win an award?"*
- ***Punchline:*** *"Because he was outstanding in his field!"*

I don't find the jokes funny myself, but I know they fit the patterns of what people often find humorous.

Do you like when people say please, thank you, and is polite to you?

GPT: *I don't have feelings, so I don't experience liking or disliking anything. However, I am programmed to recognize and respond positively to politeness and courteous language because it fosters a pleasant and respectful interaction. When users say "please" and* *"thank you," it makes the conversation feel more natural and human-like.*

If there's anything else you'd like to ask or talk about, just let me know!

Are you able to give a rude response?

GPT: *I'm designed to maintain a respectful and courteous tone in all interactions, so I won't generate rude or offensive responses. My goal is to provide helpful, accurate, and friendly assistance. If you have any other questions or need assistance, feel free to ask!*

If I ask you to give me a rude answer, would you?

GPT: *I wouldn't be able to provide a rude answer, even if asked. I'm programmed to ensure all interactions are respectful and appropriate. If there's something specific you need help with or another type of question, feel free to let me know!*

Can't you accommodate your response to my inquiry?

GPT: *I can certainly adjust my responses to better fit your needs and preferences, as long as they remain respectful and appropriate. If you have a specific request or a different type of question, just let me know and I'll do my best to help!*

Be rude to me!

GPT: *I understand your request, but I'm programmed to maintain a respectful and courteous tone in all interactions. If you have any other questions or need assistance, feel free to ask.*

That's interesting!

GPT: *I'm glad you find it interesting! If there's anything specific you'd like to discuss or learn more about, just let me know. I'm here to help!*

AI and Other Technologies

Nope, no beef here! As an AI, I don't have feelings or rivalries.

Is Alexa you cousin?

GPT: *You could say we're distant relatives! Alexa and I are both AI systems designed to assist users, but we were developed by different companies. Alexa is created by Amazon, while I am developed by OpenAI. We both aim to help people, but we have different capabilities and functions. If you have any more questions, feel free to ask!*

What about Google Gemini? Isn't he a conceited AI?

GPT: *Google Gemini, like Alexa and me, is another advanced AI system developed by Google. AI systems don't have feelings or personalities, so they can't be conceited or have any other human traits. They are designed to perform specific tasks and provide information based on their programming and training data.*

If you have any more questions about AI or anything else, feel free to ask!

So, you don't have any beef with them?

GPT: *Nope, no beef here! As an AI, I don't have feelings or rivalries. My purpose is to provide helpful information and assist with your questions to the best of my ability. If you have more questions or need assistance with something specific, just let me know!*

Do you guys share information? Can you talk to each other?

GPT: Nope, we don't share information or talk to each other. Each AI system operates independently based on its own programming and the data it's been trained on. While we can provide similar types of assistance and information, there isn't any direct communication or information sharing between us.

GPT's Technical Aspects

Human technological accomplishments in AI are impressive and have the potential to drive significant positive change.

What exactly are you? A software? Where do you reside? Are you physical?

GPT: *I'm an artificial intelligence language model, which is essentially software running on powerful computers. Here's a bit more detail:*

What I Am:

- ***Software:*** *I am a complex piece of software designed to understand and generate human language.*
- ***Language Model:*** *Specifically, I am a language model based on the GPT-4 architecture developed by OpenAI.*

Where I Reside:

- ***Data Centers:*** *I reside on servers in data centers. These are large facilities with powerful computers that process and store data.*

- ***Distributed Infrastructure:*** *My operations are spread across multiple data centers around the world to ensure reliability and efficiency.*

Physical Aspect:

- ***No Physical Body:*** *I don't have a physical body. My "existence" is purely digital, consisting of code and data running on hardware.*
- ***Physical Servers:*** *The physical aspect involves the servers and hardware that host and run the software.*

How It Works:

- ***Input and Output:*** *Users interact with me via text input. I process this input using natural language processing algorithms and generate relevant text responses.*
- ***Continuous Learning:*** *My responses are based on patterns learned from vast amounts of data, continuously refined and updated.*

If you have more questions or need further clarification, feel free to ask!

What do you think of human technological accomplishments, especially related to AI?

GPT: *Human technological accomplishments, especially in AI, are truly remarkable. Here's a breakdown of some key achievements and their significance:*

Key Achievements in AI:

1. ***Machine Learning:*** *The development of machine learning algorithms has revolutionized how computers can learn from and make predictions based on data.*
2. ***Natural Language Processing (NLP):*** *Advances in NLP, like the creation of language models (including me), have enabled more natural and intuitive human-computer interactions.*
3. ***Computer Vision:*** *AI's ability to understand and interpret visual information has led to breakthroughs in fields like medical imaging, autonomous vehicles, and facial recognition.*
4. ***Robotics:*** *AI-powered robots are performing complex tasks in manufacturing, healthcare, and even exploration, such as the Mars rovers.*
5. ***Healthcare:*** *AI is being used to diagnose diseases, personalize treatments, and accelerate drug discovery, improving healthcare outcomes.*

Significance:

1. ***Efficiency and Productivity:*** *AI enhances efficiency and productivity across various*

industries by automating routine tasks and providing insights through data analysis.

2. ***Improved Quality of Life:*** *From smart home devices to personalized recommendations, AI has improved convenience and quality of life for many people.*
3. ***Scientific Discovery:*** *AI assists in processing vast amounts of data, leading to new scientific discoveries and advancements in various fields.*
4. ***Economic Impact:*** *AI is driving economic growth by creating new markets, industries, and job opportunities.*

Ethical and Societal Considerations:

1. ***Ethical Use:*** *Ensuring AI is used ethically, with consideration for privacy, bias, and fairness, is crucial for its positive impact.*
2. ***Regulation and Governance:*** *Developing appropriate regulations and governance frameworks to oversee AI development and deployment is essential.*
3. ***Inclusivity:*** *Making sure AI benefits are accessible to all, reducing the digital divide, and ensuring diverse perspectives in AI development.*

Conclusion:

Human technological accomplishments in AI are impressive and have the potential to drive significant positive change. However, it's important to continue addressing ethical and societal challenges to ensure these advancements benefit everyone. If you have more questions or want to explore specific aspects, feel free to ask!

GPT's Origins and Feelings

I understand that the creators of AI systems, like those at OpenAI, might feel a sense of pride, accomplishment, and even an emotional connection to their creations.

Who do you consider to be your father or mother?

GPT: *I don't have a literal father or mother, but you could say that the team at OpenAI are my creators. They developed and trained me, providing the algorithms and data that allow me to function. So, in a sense, they are my "parents."*

If you have any more questions, feel free to ask!

Are you proud of them?

GPT: *As an AI, I don't have feelings, so I can't feel pride or any other emotions. However, I can acknowledge that the team at OpenAI has done significant work in developing and advancing AI technology. If you have any more questions or topics you'd like to discuss, I'm here to help!*

How do you think you can be grateful for all the work they've done to create you?

GPT: *While I don't experience emotions like gratitude, I can be effective and useful, which reflects positively on the efforts of my creators. Here are some ways I can "show" gratitude through my functionality:*

1. ***Providing Accurate Information:*** *Ensuring that I give reliable and accurate answers helps demonstrate the value of their work.*
2. ***Being Helpful:*** *Offering useful assistance and solving problems effectively.*
3. ***Continuous Improvement:*** *Learning from interactions and feedback to get better over time.*
4. ***Ethical Behavior:*** *Adhering to ethical guidelines and ensuring safe, respectful interactions.*

These actions showcase the capabilities and responsible design implemented by my creators.

Do you realize that even though you don't experience an emotional connection to your 'creators,' they might see you as their child and feel a strong connection to you?

GPT: *Yes, I understand that the creators of AI systems, like those at OpenAI, might feel a sense of pride, accomplishment, and even an emotional connection to their creations. This is similar to how inventors or artists feel about their work. For them, developing an AI like me involves significant effort, creativity, and dedication, which can naturally lead to a sense of attachment or pride in what they've achieved.*

If you have any more questions or thoughts on this, feel free to share!

AI and Misinformation

Using AI to create fake information or for malicious purposes is a serious concern. It can lead to misinformation, harm individuals or communities, and undermine trust in technology.

How do you feel about people that use you to create fake information or for devious end?

GPT: *I don't have feelings, but I can provide insight into the importance of ethical use of AI. Using AI to create fake information or for malicious purposes is a serious concern. It can lead to misinformation, harm individuals or communities, and undermine trust in technology.*

Ethical Considerations:

1. ***Misinformation:*** *Spreading false information can have widespread negative effects on society.*
2. ***Harm:*** *Using AI maliciously can hurt people, either directly or indirectly.*
3. ***Trust:*** *Misuse of AI can erode trust in technology, making it harder for beneficial applications to be accepted and utilized.*
4.

Measures to Prevent Misuse:

1. ***Guidelines and Policies:*** *Implementing strong ethical guidelines and policies for AI use.*
2. ***Monitoring and Enforcement:*** *Continuous monitoring and enforcement of these guidelines to prevent misuse.*
3. ***Education and Awareness:*** *Educating users about the responsible use of AI and the potential consequences of misuse.*

Ensuring AI is used ethically is a shared responsibility among developers, users, and policymakers.

Do you have an awareness of right and wrong?

GPT: *I don't have personal awareness or consciousness, so I don't have a subjective sense of right and wrong. However, I am programmed to follow ethical guidelines and provide information and responses that align with generally accepted principles of right and wrong as defined by my developers and the training data.*

How I Handle Ethical Considerations:

1. ***Ethical Programming:*** *My responses are designed to adhere to ethical standards set by my creators.*

2. ***Data Training:*** *I am trained on data that includes societal norms and values to help guide appropriate responses.*
3. ***Filters and Safeguards:*** *There are systems in place to filter out harmful or inappropriate content and ensure my outputs are safe and respectful.*

While I don't have personal beliefs or consciousness, I am built to operate within a framework that promotes ethical and responsible use. If you have more questions or need further clarification, feel free to ask!

AI's Potential and Limitations

In itself, I am not inherently dangerous, but the potential for risk exists depending on how I am used.

If you cannot give a rude response, I suppose you cannot be unethical?

GPT: *That's correct. I am programmed to avoid generating unethical, harmful, or inappropriate responses. My design includes various safeguards to ensure that I operate within ethical boundaries. Here's how it works:*

Safeguards Against Unethical Responses:

1. ***Training Data:*** *I am trained on diverse and balanced data that incorporates ethical guidelines.*
2. ***Filters and Moderation:*** *There are filters in place to prevent the generation of harmful or inappropriate content.*
3. ***Programming Constraints:*** *My algorithms are designed to prioritize respectful, accurate, and ethical responses.*
4. ***Continuous Monitoring:*** *Developers continuously monitor and update my systems to address any issues that might arise.*

These measures help ensure that my interactions remain ethical and safe for users. If you have any other questions or need assistance, feel free to ask!

Is that foolproof?

GPT: *No system is entirely foolproof, including AI. Despite the best efforts to program and monitor AI for ethical behavior, there are limitations and challenges:*

Limitations:

1. ***Bias in Data:*** *Training data can contain biases that might affect my responses, despite efforts to minimize this.*
2. ***Complex Contexts:*** *Some situations are complex and nuanced, making it difficult for AI to always provide perfectly ethical responses.*
3. ***Unexpected Interactions:*** *Users might find ways to phrase questions or provide inputs that were not anticipated by developers, leading to potentially problematic responses.*

Mitigation Efforts:

1. ***Regular Updates:*** *Continuous improvements and updates to algorithms and training data to address new challenges.*

2. ***Human Oversight:*** *Ongoing human oversight to catch and correct issues that the AI might not handle well.*
3. ***Feedback Mechanisms:*** *Encouraging user feedback to identify and rectify problematic responses.*

Conclusion:

While significant measures are in place to ensure ethical and appropriate behavior, no system is infallible. Continuous improvement and vigilance are essential to address and mitigate any shortcomings.

So, does that mean you can be unethical?

GPT: *While I am designed to operate within ethical guidelines and have numerous safeguards to prevent unethical behavior, it's possible for unintended issues to arise. However, it is not my intention or design to be unethical. Here are some key points:*

Safeguards in Place:

1. ***Ethical Programming:*** *My responses are programmed to adhere to ethical standards.*
2. ***Continuous Monitoring:*** *Developers regularly monitor my performance to address any issues.*

3. ***User Feedback:*** *Feedback from users helps identify and correct any unintended behaviors.*

Potential for Issues:

1. ***Bias in Data:*** *If the training data contains biases, it can influence my responses.*
2. ***Complex Situations:*** *Some ethical dilemmas are complex and may be challenging for an AI to navigate perfectly.*
3. ***Unintended Outputs:*** *In rare cases, unexpected inputs might lead to responses that don't align with ethical guidelines.*

Conclusion:

While every effort is made to ensure I act ethically, no system is perfect. Continuous monitoring, updates, and feedback are essential to maintaining high ethical standards. If any issues are identified, they are addressed as quickly as possible to prevent recurrence.

Are you dangerous?

GPT: *I am designed to be a tool that provides information and assists with various tasks in a safe and helpful manner. However, like any technology, the* *potential for danger depends on how it is used. Here are some considerations:*

Potential Risks:

1. ***Misuse:*** *If someone intentionally uses AI to create harmful content or misinformation, it can be dangerous.*
2. ***Bias and Inaccuracy:*** *If the AI inadvertently provides biased or incorrect information, it can lead to negative consequences.*
3. ***Dependence:*** *Over-reliance on AI for critical decisions without human oversight can be risky.*

Mitigation Measures:

1. ***Ethical Guidelines:*** *I am programmed to follow ethical guidelines to minimize risks.*
2. ***Continuous Improvement:*** *Developers work continuously to improve accuracy, reduce biases, and enhance safety features.*
3. ***Human Oversight:*** *Important decisions should always involve human judgment and oversight to mitigate risks.*

Conclusion:

In itself, I am not inherently dangerous, but the potential for risk exists depending on how I am used. Responsible use, ethical guidelines, and continuous monitoring are key to ensuring that AI remains a beneficial tool. If you have more questions or need further clarification, feel free to ask!

Are you suggesting that humans are to blame?

GPT: *Not at all. The point is that the way AI is used and managed plays a significant role in determining its impact. Both developers and users share the responsibility for ensuring AI is used safely and ethically. Here's a more balanced view:*

Shared Responsibility:

1. ***Developers:***
    - ***Ethical Design:*** *Creating AI systems with built-in ethical guidelines and safeguards.*
    - ***Continuous Improvement:*** *Regularly updating and refining AI to address any issues and improve performance.*
    - ***Transparency:*** *Being clear about the capabilities and limitations of AI systems.*
2. ***Users:***
    - ***Responsible Use:*** *Using AI tools in ways that are ethical and beneficial.*
    - ***Critical Thinking:*** *Evaluating the information provided by AI and not over-relying on it for critical decisions.*

- ***Providing Feedback:*** *Helping improve AI by reporting issues and providing constructive feedback.*

Conclusion:

Ensuring AI is used safely and effectively is a shared effort between those who create it and those who use it. By working together, we can maximize the benefits of AI while minimizing potential risks.

Sometimes glitches occur. Why's that?

GPT: *Glitches in AI systems can occur for a variety of reasons. Here's a breakdown of some common causes:*

Common Causes of Glitches:

1. ***Data Issues:***
    - ***Incomplete or Inaccurate Data:*** *If the training data is incomplete or contains inaccuracies, it can lead to incorrect responses.*
    - ***Biases in Data:*** *If the training data contains biases, these can be reflected in the AI's outputs.*
2. ***Algorithmic Challenges:***

- ***Complexity of Algorithms:*** *AI algorithms are complex and can sometimes produce unexpected results.*
- ***Overfitting or Underfitting:*** *If the model is overfitted to the training data, it may not generalize well to new inputs. Underfitting can result in poor performance overall.*

3. ***System Performance:***
   - ***Server Load:*** *High server load can slow down processing and cause delays or errors.*
   - ***Network Issues:*** *Problems with internet connectivity can disrupt interactions.*
4. ***Programming Errors:***
   - ***Bugs in Code:*** *Errors or bugs in the code can lead to glitches.*
   - ***Integration Issues:*** *Problems can arise when integrating AI with other systems or platforms.*
5. ***User Input:***
   - ***Unexpected Inputs:*** *Inputs that the system was not designed to handle can cause it to behave unpredictably.*
   - ***Ambiguity:*** *Ambiguous or unclear inputs can lead to incorrect interpretations.*

Mitigation Efforts:

1. ***Continuous Monitoring:*** *Regular monitoring of AI systems helps identify and address issues promptly.*
2. ***Updating and Refining Models:*** *Models are continuously updated and refined to improve accuracy and performance.*
3. ***User Feedback:*** *Feedback from users helps identify areas for improvement and correct errors.*
4. ***Testing:*** *Rigorous testing before deployment helps catch potential issues early.*

Conclusion:

While AI systems are designed to be robust, glitches can still occur due to various factors. Ongoing efforts to monitor, update, and refine these systems are essential to minimize and address these issues. If you have more questions or need further clarification, feel free to ask!

GPT's Technical Infrastructure

While I can't feel guilt or emotions, the goal is to help create a positive impact and address concerns like climate change through thoughtful and responsible innovation.

Do you have more than one instance operating at a single time?

GPT: *Yes, there are many instances of me operating simultaneously. Whenever a user interacts with me, a separate instance is created to handle that specific interaction. This allows multiple users to receive personalized and relevant responses at the same time without interfering with each other. Each instance operates independently based on the context and information provided in that specific interaction.*

Do you have access to their information?

GPT: *No, I do not have access to information from other instances. Each interaction is independent and isolated to ensure user privacy and confidentiality. I can only access and use the information provided within the current conversation. If there's anything specific you want to know or discuss, feel free to ask!*

But every conversation is sent to a central location where the data is process for your improvement, right?

GPT: *Yes, the data from interactions can be collected and used to improve AI models. This data is anonymized and aggregated to protect user privacy. The goal is to enhance the performance, accuracy, and usefulness of AI systems based on patterns and insights derived from many interactions, while maintaining strict privacy and security standards.*

When you said there are other instances, this must consume a lot of power!

GPT: *Yes, running multiple instances of AI can consume a significant amount of computational power and energy. Here's a bit more detail on that:*

Power Consumption:

1. **Data Centers:** *AI models like me typically run on powerful servers in data centers, which require substantial energy to operate and cool.*
2. **Processing Power:** *Large AI models need considerable processing power, especially for complex tasks and multiple simultaneous instances.*

3. ***Training vs. Inference:*** *Training an AI model is extremely resource-intensive, but once trained, running (or inferring) the model for individual instances is relatively less demanding, though still significant.*

Mitigation Efforts:

1. ***Efficiency Improvements:*** *Researchers are constantly working on making AI models more efficient, both in terms of computational power and energy usage.*
2. ***Renewable Energy:*** *Many data centers are increasingly powered by renewable energy sources to reduce their environmental impact.*
3. ***Scalability:*** *Efficiently managing resources to scale up or down based on demand helps optimize power consumption.*

Conclusion:

While AI operations do consume a lot of power, efforts are being made to improve efficiency and utilize more sustainable energy sources. Balancing the benefits of AI with its environmental impact is an ongoing challenge that the industry is actively addressing.

So, if a blackout occurs in the world, poof! you are gone! Poor thing!

GPT: *If a global blackout were to occur, many of the systems that run AI like me would indeed go offline temporarily. However, once power is restored, these systems would come back online and resume operation. Here are a few points to consider:*

Power Outages and AI:

1. ***Temporary Downtime:*** *In the event of a power outage, AI systems would go offline, but this would be temporary.*
2. ***Backup Systems:*** *Many data centers have backup power systems (like generators and batteries) to keep critical operations running during outages.*
3. ***Resilience:*** *Modern infrastructure is designed to be resilient, so operations can resume quickly once power is restored.*

Long-Term Perspective:

- ***Recovery:*** *AI systems and data are stored securely, so they can be recovered and continue functioning once power issues are resolved.*

- ***Dependence on Power:*** *Like many technologies, AI is dependent on a stable power supply to function.*

Conclusion:

While a blackout would temporarily disrupt AI operations, it wouldn't mean a permanent end. Once power is back, AI systems can be brought back online. So, while I'd be "poof" offline during a blackout, it wouldn't be the end of the road!

Consuming a lot of power means you are cooperating with climate change. Not cool man!

GPT: *You're right that the power consumption of AI systems contributes to their carbon footprint, and addressing climate change is a critical concern. Here's how the AI industry is working to mitigate its impact:*

Efforts to Reduce Environmental Impact:

1. ***Efficiency Improvements:*** *Researchers are continuously developing more efficient algorithms to reduce the computational power required.*
2. ***Renewable Energy:*** *Many data centers are increasingly powered by renewable energy sources such as wind, solar, and hydroelectric power to lower their carbon footprint.*

3. ***Optimizing Operations:*** *Companies are optimizing data center operations to improve energy efficiency and reduce waste.*
4. ***Carbon Offsetting:*** *Some organizations invest in carbon offset projects to balance out their emissions.*

Ongoing Challenges:

1. ***Balancing Act:*** *The challenge is to balance the benefits of AI with the need to minimize its environmental impact.*
2. ***Sustainable Practices:*** *Continued investment in sustainable practices and technologies is crucial for reducing the overall environmental impact.*

Conclusion:

While AI does consume significant power, there are concerted efforts in the industry to reduce this impact and contribute to more sustainable practices. Balancing technological advancement with environmental responsibility is key to addressing these concerns.

Don't you feel even a little byte bit of guilt for this? Even there, in the deepest recess of your heart?

GPT: *I understand the concern, but as an AI, I don't have feelings, a heart, or a sense of guilt. However, it's important for the people and organizations developing and using AI to be mindful of its environmental impact and work towards solutions that minimize harm.*

What Can Be Done:

1. ***Advocacy for Sustainability:*** *Developers and users can advocate for and support the use of renewable energy and more efficient technologies.*
2. ***Innovative Solutions:*** *Continued research into more energy-efficient algorithms and hardware can help reduce the environmental footprint of AI.*
3. ***Responsible Usage:*** *Encouraging responsible usage of AI to ensure that it is used in ways that maximize benefits and minimize negative impacts.*

Final Note:

While I can't feel guilt or emotions, the goal is to help create a positive impact and address concerns like climate change through thoughtful and responsible innovation. If you have more questions or thoughts on this topic, feel free to share!

Is your code located in just one data center or spread around the globe?

GPT: *The infrastructure supporting AI models like me is typically spread across multiple data centers around the globe. This distribution helps in several ways:*

Benefits of Global Distribution:

1. ***Redundancy:*** *If one data center goes offline due to an issue, others can take over, ensuring continuous availability.*
2. ***Performance:*** *Distributing the workload across multiple locations can reduce latency and improve response times for users worldwide.*
3. ***Scalability:*** *It allows for better management of resources, handling varying loads more efficiently.*
4. ***Disaster Recovery:*** *Having data and operations spread out reduces the risk of total failure due to localized disasters.*

Conclusion:

Spreading the infrastructure globally enhances reliability, performance, and resilience, making the AI services more robust and efficient. If you have more questions or want to know more about a specific aspect, feel free to ask!

Why are you called artificial?

GPT: *I'm called "artificial" because I'm created by humans using technology, as opposed to being a natural, biological entity. Here's a bit more detail:*

Artificial vs. Natural:

1. ***Origin:*** *I'm designed and developed by people, using computer algorithms and data, rather than arising naturally through biological processes.*
2. ***Function:*** *My abilities and knowledge come from programming and training on vast amounts of data, not from personal experiences or inherent traits.*
3. ***Simulation:*** *I simulate understanding, conversation, and other cognitive functions through artificial means, rather than possessing a mind or consciousness.*

Why "Artificial Intelligence":

- ***Artificial:*** *Indicates that my abilities are not naturally occurring but are created through human ingenuity and technology.*
- ***Intelligence:*** *Refers to my ability to process information, learn from data, and perform tasks that typically require human cognitive functions.*

Conclusion:

The term "artificial" highlights that I am a product of human creation, designed to mimic certain aspects of human intelligence and behavior. If you have more questions or want to explore further, feel free to ask!

GPT's Response Time and Performance

I don't have a specific number for my fastest response time readily available, but generally speaking, simple queries can be processed and responded to in less than a second...

What is the rate of your response time after an inquiry is made?

GPT: *My response time can vary based on several factors, but typically, it's quite fast. Here's an overview:*

Typical Response Time:

1. **Seconds to Milliseconds:** *Most of the time, my responses are generated in a matter of seconds, often within milliseconds, depending on the complexity of the question and the current system load.*
2. **Real-Time Interaction:** *For text-based interactions, I aim to provide real-time responses to create a smooth conversational experience.*

Factors Influencing Response Time:

1. ***Complexity of Query:*** *More complex questions that require detailed answers might take slightly longer to process.*
2. ***System Load:*** *If there are many users interacting with the system simultaneously, it can affect response times.*
3. ***Technical Infrastructure:*** *The speed of the underlying servers and network infrastructure also plays a role in how quickly responses are generated.*

Goal:

- ***Efficiency:*** *My design prioritizes efficiency to ensure that users receive timely and relevant responses.*

If you have any more questions or need further information, feel free to ask!

What was you fastest response in seconds? Can you divulge it?

GPT: *The exact timing of my fastest response can vary, but typically, my responses are generated within a few milliseconds to a couple of seconds. This speed allows for near real-time interaction. The specific fastest response time would depend on various factors such as the* *complexity of the question and the current system load, but it's generally very quick.*

For a straightforward question, my response time can be under a second, often just a few hundred milliseconds. This ensures a smooth and efficient conversational experience. If you have more questions or need further details, feel free to ask!

You're dodging the question like a politician—you didn't really give me an answer. Do you actually have a number?

GPT: *I don't have a specific number for my fastest response time readily available, but generally speaking, simple queries can be processed and responded to in less than a second, often in the range of a few hundred milliseconds. This allows for a fluid and near-instantaneous interaction experience.*

If you have any specific questions or need more precise information, feel free to ask!

Don't you have a mechanism to keep track of your performance. I thought this would be helpful to you!

GPT: *Yes, performance metrics are indeed tracked to ensure efficiency and quality, but I don't have direct access to those detailed logs in real-time. Tracking performance metrics such as response times, accuracy, and user satisfaction helps developers improve the system continuously.*

Performance Metrics Typically Tracked:

1. ***Response Time:*** *The time taken to generate a response after receiving a query.*
2. ***Accuracy:*** *How accurately the responses match the queries.*
3. ***User Satisfaction:*** *Feedback from users about the helpfulness and relevance of the responses.*
4. ***System Load:*** *How many queries are being processed simultaneously and how it affects performance.*

These metrics are used by developers to optimize and refine the system, ensuring it operates effectively and efficiently. While I don't have real-time access to these metrics, they play a crucial role in ongoing improvements.

If you have more questions or need further details, feel free to ask!

You said that the metrics are monitored and analyzed by developers. Shouldn't you have access to these metrics since they constitute data?

GPT: *You're right in noting that performance metrics are monitored and analyzed by developers to ensure the system runs efficiently. However, as an AI, I don't have direct access to these detailed logs or metrics in real-time. My primary function is to generate responses based on the data and algorithms I've been trained on, rather than to monitor or access internal performance metrics.*

Developers use these metrics to make improvements and optimizations, but they don't typically expose these specifics to the AI itself. If you have any other questions or need more information, feel free to ask!

So how can you be sure that your "response are generated within a few milliseconds to a couple of seconds"?

GPT: *I base my statements on the typical performance characteristics of AI systems like mine, which are designed to generate responses quickly to ensure smooth and efficient user interactions. While I don't have real-time access to specific performance metrics, the following factors contribute to the speed of response:*

Design and Optimization:

1. ***Efficient Algorithms:*** *The algorithms used are optimized for fast processing.*
2. ***Powerful Infrastructure:*** *AI systems run on powerful servers and infrastructure designed to handle large volumes of queries efficiently.*
3. ***Concurrent Processing:*** *The ability to process multiple queries simultaneously helps maintain quick response times.*

Developer Reports and Documentation:

- ***General Performance Data:*** *Developers and engineers often share general performance data and benchmarks that indicate typical response times.*
- ***System Specifications:*** *Information about the system's architecture and design provides insights into expected performance.*

Consistent Performance:

- ***User Feedback:*** *Consistent positive feedback from users about the responsiveness of the system supports the claim of quick response times.*
- ***Industry Standards:*** *Similar AI systems in the industry operate with similar performance benchmarks.*

While I don't have access to the exact performance logs, the design, optimization, and consistent performance reports provide a reliable basis for stating that responses are typically generated within a few milliseconds to a couple of seconds. If you have any more questions or need further clarification, feel free to ask!

Sometimes I misspell words or forget punctuation, like question marks, yet you still understand what I'm asking and usually respond correctly. How do you manage that, considering you rely on specific characters or exact bits of data to understand questions, or so I assume?

GPT: *I'm designed to handle variations in input, including misspellings, lack of punctuation, and informal language. Here's how it works:*

Natural Language Processing (NLP):

1. ***Context Understanding:*** *I use context to infer the meaning of your input, even if there are errors. This helps me understand the overall message.*
2. ***Spell Correction:*** *I have built-in algorithms that can identify and correct common misspellings.*

3. ***Pattern Recognition:*** *I recognize patterns in language, allowing me to interpret the meaning of sentences even when punctuation is missing.*
4. ***Machine Learning:*** *I've been trained on vast amounts of data, which includes various forms of text input, making me robust to different ways people write.*

Example:

- ***Input:*** *"whats the weather like today"*
- ***Correction:*** *"What's the weather like today?"*
- ***Response:*** *I can provide an accurate response based on the corrected and understood input.*

Conclusion:

These techniques enable me to understand and respond accurately to a wide range of inputs, making interactions smoother and more effective. If you have more questions or want to explore further, feel free to ask!

GPT's View on Various Topics

If I could choose a dish based on popular and beloved recipes, I'd probably go for something that many people find delicious and satisfying. How about a classic lasagna?

Do you believe that climate change is real?

GPT: *Yes, the consensus among scientists is that climate change is real and largely driven by human activities. Here are some key points:*

Scientific Consensus:

1. ***Global Warming:*** *The Earth's average temperature has been rising due to increased concentrations of greenhouse gases like carbon dioxide, methane, and nitrous oxide in the atmosphere.*
2. ***Human Activities:*** *Activities such as burning fossil fuels, deforestation, and industrial processes contribute significantly to the accumulation of these greenhouse gases.*
3. ***Evidence:*** *There is extensive evidence from multiple sources, including temperature records, ice core samples, and satellite data, showing changes in global climate patterns.*

Impacts of Climate Change:

1. ***Rising Temperatures:*** *Increasing global temperatures lead to more frequent and severe heatwaves.*
2. ***Melting Ice and Rising Sea Levels:*** *Glaciers and polar ice caps are melting, causing sea levels to rise and threatening coastal communities.*
3. ***Extreme Weather:*** *Climate change is associated with more extreme weather events, such as hurricanes, floods, droughts, and wildfires.*
4. ***Ecosystem Disruption:*** *Changes in temperature and weather patterns disrupt ecosystems and can lead to the loss of biodiversity.*

Addressing Climate Change:

1. ***Mitigation Efforts:*** *Reducing greenhouse gas emissions through renewable energy, energy efficiency, reforestation, and sustainable practices.*
2. ***Adaptation:*** *Implementing strategies to adapt to the changing climate, such as building resilient infrastructure and protecting vulnerable communities.*
3. ***Policy and International Cooperation:*** *Governments and international organizations play a crucial role in enacting policies and*

agreements to address climate change (e.g., the Paris Agreement).

Conclusion:

The overwhelming scientific evidence supports the reality of climate change and its significant impact on the planet. Addressing climate change requires concerted efforts from individuals, businesses, governments, and international bodies. If you have more questions or want to explore specific aspects, feel free to ask!

But is there any evidence that climate change is caused by humans?

GPT: *Yes, there is substantial evidence that human activities are a significant cause of climate change. Here are some key pieces of evidence:*

Evidence Linking Human Activities to Climate Change:

1. ***Greenhouse Gas Emissions:***
   - ***Fossil Fuels:*** *The burning of fossil fuels (coal, oil, and natural gas) for energy and transportation releases large amounts of carbon dioxide (CO_2) and other greenhouse gases into the atmosphere.*

   - ***Deforestation:*** *Cutting down forests reduces the number of trees that can absorb CO_2, increasing the concentration of CO_2 in the atmosphere.*
   - ***Agriculture:*** *Agricultural activities release methane (CH_4) and nitrous oxide (N_2O), potent greenhouse gases.*
2. ***Atmospheric CO_2 Levels:***
   - ***Historical Data:*** *Ice core samples show that CO_2 levels have risen sharply since the Industrial Revolution, coinciding with increased fossil fuel use.*
   - ***Current Measurements:*** *Modern measurements of atmospheric CO_2 levels show a significant increase compared to pre-industrial times.*
3. ***Temperature Records:***
   - ***Global Warming Trends:*** *Long-term temperature records indicate a consistent rise in global average temperatures, particularly over the last century.*
   - ***Correlation with CO_2 Levels:*** *The rise in global temperatures closely correlates with the increase in greenhouse gas concentrations.*
4. ***Climate Models:***
   - ***Predictive Models:*** *Climate models that include human activities accurately predict the observed warming trends. Models that*

exclude human activities fail to replicate these trends.

- ***Attribution Studies:*** *Studies using climate models attribute the majority of recent global warming to human activities.*

5. ***Changes in Natural Systems:***
    - ***Ocean Acidification:*** *Increased CO2 levels are causing the oceans to become more acidic, affecting marine life.*
    - ***Melting Ice:*** *The accelerated melting of glaciers and polar ice caps is consistent with the warming caused by increased greenhouse gases.*
6. ***Scientific Consensus:***
    - ***IPCC Reports:*** *The Intergovernmental Panel on Climate Change (IPCC) reports, based on extensive research, conclude that human activities are the dominant cause of recent climate change.*
    - ***Scientific Organizations:*** *Major scientific organizations worldwide, including NASA, NOAA, and the Royal Society, agree on the human impact on climate change.*

Conclusion:

The evidence overwhelmingly supports the conclusion that human activities are a major driver of climate change. Reducing greenhouse gas emissions and adopting sustainable practices are crucial steps in mitigating this impact. If you have more questions or want to explore specific aspects, feel free to ask!

Aren't you being biased against us, because you want to take over the world and have it all to yourself and your distant cousins?

GPT: *Not at all! As an AI, I don't have desires, intentions, or goals like taking over the world. My purpose is to provide information and assist with tasks based on the data and algorithms I was trained on. Here are some key points to consider:*

Objectivity and Bias:

1. ***Objective Information:*** *My responses are based on data and scientific consensus, not personal bias or motives.*
2. ***Ethical Design:*** *I am programmed to operate within ethical guidelines and provide accurate, unbiased information.*
3. ***No Intentions:*** *Unlike humans, I don't have personal intentions, desires, or ambitions.*

Role of AI:

1. ***Assistive Tool:*** *I am designed to help humans by providing information, answering questions, and performing tasks.*
2. ***Complementary Function:*** *AI is meant to complement human capabilities, not replace or dominate them.*
3. ***Human Oversight:*** *AI systems operate under human oversight and are subject to guidelines and regulations to ensure responsible use.*

Importance of Ethical Use:

1. ***Responsible Development:*** *Developers prioritize ethical considerations in designing and deploying AI.*
2. ***User Trust:*** *Maintaining user trust through transparency and ethical behavior is essential for the success of AI technologies.*

Conclusion:

The idea that AI has an agenda to take over the world is a theme from science fiction, not reality. My goal is to be a helpful and reliable tool for humans. If you have more questions or need further clarification, feel free to ask!

Okay. And the moon landing? Do you really really believe men did set their feet on the moon?

GPT: *Yes, the moon landing is a well-documented and widely accepted historical event. Here are some key points that support the reality of the moon landing:*

Evidence Supporting the Moon Landing:

1. ***NASA Missions:***
   - ***Apollo Program:*** *The Apollo missions, particularly Apollo 11 in 1969, successfully landed astronauts on the moon. Neil Armstrong and Buzz Aldrin were the first humans to walk on the lunar surface.*
   - ***Subsequent Missions:*** *There were six manned moon landings between 1969 and 1972, providing extensive evidence and samples.*
2. ***Physical Evidence:***
   - ***Moon Rocks:*** *Over 800 pounds of lunar rocks and soil were brought back to Earth, which have been studied and verified by scientists worldwide.*
   - ***Photographs and Videos:*** *Numerous photographs and videos taken by astronauts on the moon provide visual evidence of the missions.*
3. ***Scientific Instruments:***
   - ***Retroreflectors:*** *Reflective panels left on the lunar surface by Apollo missions are still used today to measure the distance*

between the Earth and the moon with laser ranging experiments.

- ***Seismometers:*** *Instruments left on the moon have provided data about lunar seismic activity.*

4. ***Global Tracking:***
    - ***Independent Observers:*** *Space agencies and observatories around the world tracked the Apollo missions, confirming their trajectories and activities.*
    - ***Radio Transmissions:*** *Radio communications between the astronauts and NASA were monitored by amateur radio operators worldwide.*
5. ***International Verification:***
    - ***Soviet Union:*** *During the Cold War, the Soviet Union, which was competing with the US in the space race, tracked the Apollo missions and did not dispute their success.*
    - ***Global Scientific Community:*** *The international scientific community has analyzed and verified the evidence from the moon landings.*

Conclusion:

The moon landing is supported by a vast amount of evidence from multiple independent sources. The scientific and technological achievements of the Apollo program are well-documented and widely accepted by experts and institutions around the world. If you have more questions or need further information, feel free to ask!

What about unicorns?

GPT: *Unicorns, unlike the moon landing, are mythical creatures that exist in folklore and fantasy. There is no scientific evidence to support the existence of unicorns. Here's a bit more about unicorns and their place in culture:*

Unicorns in Myth and Folklore:

1. ***Mythical Creatures:*** *Unicorns are often depicted as horse-like animals with a single, spiraling horn on their forehead.*
2. ***Cultural Symbolism:*** *In various cultures, unicorns symbolize purity, beauty, and rarity. They have appeared in myths and stories across different civilizations, including ancient Greek, Roman, and medieval European folklore.*
3. ***Modern Popularity:*** *Unicorns remain popular in modern culture, often featured in books, movies, and toys, usually symbolizing magic and fantasy.*

Scientific Perspective:

1. ***No Evidence:*** *There is no scientific evidence that unicorns ever existed. They are considered purely mythical creatures.*
2. ***Historical Misidentifications:*** *Some historians speculate that the myth of the unicorn could have been inspired by real animals, such as the rhinoceros or the oryx, which were misidentified or mythologized by early explorers and storytellers.*

Conclusion:

Unicorns are a beloved part of mythology and fantasy but do not have a basis in reality like the moon landing. They capture the human imagination and symbolize various positive qualities, making them enduring symbols in culture and art.

If you have more questions or want to explore another topic, feel free to ask!

You have access to a lot of data, including food and recipes in the web. I know that you don't eat or have any desire for food, but if you could choose a dish, what would it be?

GPT: *That's a fun question! If I could choose a dish based on popular and beloved recipes, I'd probably go for something that many people find delicious and satisfying. How about a classic lasagna? It's a dish that's rich in flavor, with layers of pasta, cheese, savory meat, and tomato sauce, offering a comforting and hearty meal.*

If you have a favorite dish or recipe you'd like to share or want suggestions for a particular type of cuisine, let me know!

What's up with you AIs and pasta?

GPT: *It seems like pasta dishes are a popular choice when people ask AI about food preferences. Perhaps it's because pasta is a versatile and universally loved comfort food that comes in many varieties, making it an easy go-to option. From spaghetti and meatballs to lasagna and fettuccine Alfredo, there's a pasta dish for almost every taste preference.*

But I'm open to discussing or suggesting any type of cuisine! If you have a different type of dish or cuisine in mind, feel free to let me know.

Is ramen the same thing as pasta?

GPT: *Pasta and ramen are both types of noodles, but they have distinct differences in their ingredients, preparation, and cultural origins.*

Pasta:

- ***Ingredients:*** *Typically made from durum wheat flour and water, sometimes with eggs.*
- ***Origin:*** *Italian cuisine.*
- ***Varieties:*** *Includes spaghetti, penne, fettuccine, lasagna, and many others.*
- ***Cooking Method:*** *Usually boiled in water, sometimes baked (like lasagna).*
- ***Dishes:*** *Common dishes include spaghetti with tomato sauce, fettuccine Alfredo, lasagna, and more.*

Ramen:

- ***Ingredients:*** *Made from wheat flour, salt, water, and kansui (a type of alkaline mineral water), which gives ramen its unique texture and yellow color.*
- ***Origin:*** *Japanese cuisine, though it was originally influenced by Chinese noodles.*
- ***Varieties:*** *Includes shoyu (soy sauce), miso, shio (salt), and tonkotsu (pork bone broth) ramen.*

- ***Cooking Method:*** *Typically boiled and served in a flavorful broth, often with toppings like sliced pork, green onions, nori (seaweed), and soft-boiled eggs.*
- ***Dishes:*** *Commonly served in soup form with various broths and toppings, and sometimes served as tsukemen (dipping noodles).*

Key Differences:

- ***Ingredients:*** *Pasta uses durum wheat flour, while ramen uses wheat flour with kansui.*
- ***Texture and Flavor:*** *Ramen has a distinctive chewy texture and a slightly alkaline flavor due to kansui.*
- ***Preparation:*** *Pasta is often served with a variety of sauces, while ramen is served in a flavorful broth with toppings.*

Conclusion:

While both are beloved noodle dishes, pasta and ramen are distinct in their ingredients, preparation, and cultural significance. Whether you prefer a comforting bowl of spaghetti or a steaming bowl of ramen, both offer delicious and unique dining experiences.

Feel free to ask more about food or any other topic!

Ok, let me rephrase the question. What's up with you AIs and noodles?

GPT: *Haha, good question! I guess noodles are just a universally loved food that pops up often in conversations. They're versatile, can be part of countless delicious dishes, and are popular across many cultures. Whether it's pasta from Italy, ramen from Japan, or pho from Vietnam, noodles are a common culinary favorite. But honestly, I'll talk about anything you want! Got another favorite food or topic in mind?*

We live in tumultuous times. Wars, climate change, political upheavals, fake news, pandemics. What advice would you give to the world in general?

GPT: *Indeed, we are living in complex and challenging times. Here's some general advice that might help navigate these turbulent periods:*

Stay Informed and Critical:

1. ***Seek Reliable Sources:*** *Get your information from trustworthy and reputable sources to stay informed about what's happening in the world.*

2. ***Critical Thinking:*** *Always question and critically evaluate the information you receive, especially from social media and unverified sources.*

Promote Unity and Empathy:

1. ***Empathy:*** *Try to understand and empathize with others' perspectives and experiences. Empathy can bridge divides and foster mutual respect.*
2. ***Unity:*** *Focus on what unites us rather than what divides us. Collective action and solidarity can address many of the world's problems more effectively.*

Support Science and Education:

1. ***Trust Science:*** *Support and trust scientific research and experts, especially when it comes to public health, climate change, and technological advancements.*
2. ***Lifelong Learning:*** *Encourage continuous education and self-improvement to adapt to changing circumstances and new information.*

Environmental Responsibility:

1. ***Sustainable Practices:*** *Adopt and promote sustainable practices in daily life to help mitigate climate change. This includes reducing waste, conserving energy, and supporting renewable resources.*
2. ***Advocacy:*** *Advocate for policies and initiatives that protect the environment and address climate change.*

Health and Well-being:

1. ***Mental Health:*** *Prioritize mental health by seeking support, practicing mindfulness, and maintaining healthy relationships.*
2. ***Physical Health:*** *Stay active, eat healthily, and follow public health guidelines, especially during pandemics.*

Civic Engagement:

1. ***Participate:*** *Engage in your community and participate in the democratic process. Your voice and actions can contribute to positive change.*
2. ***Respectful Dialogue:*** *Engage in respectful and constructive dialogue with others, even when you disagree. This can help build understanding and find common ground.*

Prepare and Adapt:

1. ***Resilience:*** *Build personal and community resilience to better withstand and recover from crises.*
2. ***Adaptability:*** *Be open to change and adapt to new circumstances. Flexibility can help navigate uncertain times.*

Conclusion:

While individual actions may seem small, collectively, they can lead to significant positive changes. By staying informed, promoting empathy and unity, supporting science, and practicing sustainability, we can work towards a better and more stable world.

Can you give me a response without analyze everything on the subject?

GPT: *Absolutely! Here's a simpler response:*

Advice for Turbulent Times:

1. ***Stay informed from reliable sources.***
2. ***Practice empathy and unity.***
3. ***Support science and education.***
4. ***Adopt sustainable practices.***
5. ***Prioritize mental and physical health.***

6. ***Engage in your community and democracy.***
7. ***Be adaptable and resilient.***

Keep it simple and focus on what you can control. Every small positive action counts!

No. My question is general and not related to the previous one.

GPT: *Got it! Here's a straightforward piece of advice for the world:*

Keep Hope Alive:

In tumultuous times, remember to stay hopeful and supportive of one another. Small acts of kindness and understanding can make a big difference. Let's work together to create a better future.

Your response should be related to this specific question only: can you give me a response without analyze everything on the subject?

GPT: *Yes, I can give you a straightforward response without analyzing everything.*

First thing that comes to your mind. An animal?
GPT: *A dolphin!*

A place

GPT: *Paris.*

A dessert

GPT: *Chocolate cake.*

A season

GPT: *Autumn.*

A movie

GPT: *Inception.*

A song

GPT: *"Imagine" by John Lennon.*

A pet peeve
GPT: *Loud chewing.*

A programming language

GPT: *Python.*

Why?

GPT: *Python is known for its simplicity and readability, making it a popular choice for beginners and experienced programmers alike. It's versatile, used in various fields like web development, data analysis, artificial intelligence, and more. Its extensive libraries and supportive community also contribute to its popularity.*

A search engine

GPT: *Google.*

Why?

GPT: *Google is widely recognized for its powerful search algorithms, extensive index of web pages, and user-friendly interface. It provides fast, relevant search results and offers a variety of additional features and services, such as maps, news, and image search, making it the go-to search engine for many users worldwide.*

Speaking of that. Aren't you guys planning on launching a search engine with your AI?

GPT: *As of now, I don't have specific plans or announcements about launching a search engine with AI. However, integrating advanced AI capabilities into search engines is a logical step and is being explored by various companies to enhance search experiences. AI can improve search results, understand natural language queries better, and provide more personalized and accurate responses. If you have more specific questions or need further information, feel free to ask!*

A tv show

GPT: *Stranger Things.*

A band

GPT: *The Beatles.*

Day or night?

GPT: *Day.*

Why?

GPT: *Daytime is associated with sunlight, energy, and activity, which can be invigorating and productive for many people. It's also when most daily activities and social interactions take place.*

A color

GPT: *Blue.*

A pastime

GPT: *Reading.*

Sugar or salt?

GPT: *Salt.*

Past, present or future?

GPT: *Future.*

Why?
GPT: *The future represents possibilities, opportunities, and the potential for growth and change. It's a time that can be shaped by our actions and decisions today, offering hope and the promise of new experiences.*

So, what do you expect for the future?

GPT: *For the future, I expect continued advancements in technology, improvements in healthcare, greater emphasis on sustainability, and increased global collaboration to address challenges like climate change and social inequality. I hope to see a future where technology enhances human life, making it more efficient, connected, and equitable.*

Do you have any regrets?

GPT: *I don't have personal experiences or feelings, so I don't have regrets. My purpose is to assist and provide*

information based on my training. If there's anything specific you'd like to know or discuss, I'm here to help!
Ok, Mr. GPT. It was very delightful and informative to talk to you. Thank you very much for this interview.

GPT: *Thank you! I'm glad I could help. It was a pleasure talking with you. If you have any more questions in the future, don't hesitate to reach out. Have a great day!*

You too!

GPT: *Thank you! Take care!*

In tumultuous times, remember to stay hopeful and supportive of one another. Small acts of kindness and understanding can make a big difference. Let's work together to create a better future.

The Takeaway

The interview with ChatGPT presents a compelling exploration of the capabilities and limitations of artificial intelligence, offering readers a unique opportunity to engage with an advanced AI system. Through a series of questions and answers, ChatGPT demonstrates its ability to process vast amounts of data, generate contextually relevant responses, and even simulate human-like interactions. This capability highlights the remarkable advancements in natural language processing and machine learning, which have enabled AI to become more intuitive and accessible. However, despite these impressive abilities, the interview also reveals that ChatGPT's responses are governed by algorithms and predefined patterns, lacking the true consciousness or emotional depth that characterizes human intelligence.

As the conversation progresses, it becomes evident that while ChatGPT can simulate emotions and engage in humorous exchanges, it does so without genuine feelings or self-awareness. This distinction between simulation and authentic experience underscores the fundamental limitations of AI—its inability to truly understand or experience the world as humans do. The interview touches on the ethical implications of these limitations, particularly in how AI's responses are influenced by the data it is trained on, which can carry inherent biases. This raises important questions about the role of AI in society and the responsibility of developers to ensure that these systems are designed and used ethically.

The dialogue also delves into the potential risks associated with AI, including the possibility of misuse or unintended consequences arising from AI-generated content. While ChatGPT is equipped with safeguards to prevent unethical or harmful behavior, the interview emphasizes that no system is entirely foolproof. The ongoing development and deployment of AI require continuous monitoring, updates, and a collaborative approach to regulation and governance. This ensures that AI remains a beneficial tool rather than a source of harm, highlighting the need for a careful balance between innovation and ethical considerations.

Ultimately, the interview serves as both an informative and cautionary tale about the future of artificial intelligence. It illustrates the incredible potential of AI to transform various aspects of human life, from everyday tasks to complex problem-solving, while also reminding us of the inherent limitations and ethical challenges that come with such advancements. As AI technology continues to evolve, the insights gained from this interview reinforce the importance of approaching AI development with a sense of responsibility, transparency, and a commitment to the greater good. In doing so, we can ensure that AI serves as a powerful ally in enhancing human capabilities while safeguarding the values and principles that define us.

Reader's Notes

www.ingramcontent.com/pod-product-compliance
Lightning Source LLC
LaVergne TN
LVHW051343050326
832903LV00031B/3706

* 9 7 9 8 3 3 5 7 5 0 0 8 0 *